MW01489914

Inside
my
Head

By Courtney E. Butts

ZOË LIFE
PUBLISHING
WORDS TO LIVE BY

Published by:
Zoë Life Publishing
P.O. Box 871066
Canton, MI 48187 USA
www.zoelifepub.com

Author: Courtney E. Butts
Cover Design Team: Chamira Jones and Josh D. Mobley
Editor: Jessica Colvin

First U.S. Edition 2008

ISBN13 – 978-1-934363-13-3

Butts, Courtney E.
  Inside my head / by Courtney E. Butts. -- 1st U.S. ed.
     p. cm.
  ISBN 978-1-934363-13-3 (pbk.)
  I. Title.
  PS3602.U8929I57 2007
  811'.6--dc22
                         2007026875

For current information about releases by **Courtney E. Butts** or other releases from Zoë Life Publishing, visit our web site:
http://www.zoelifepub.com

Printed in the United States of America

v7 02 12 08 CB

Acknowledgements and Thank You's

Words cannot express how thankful I am for all the important people in my life.

First, I would like to thank God who gave me a second chance at life.

To my family, especially my mother, who loves me unconditionally and would do anything for me.

To Shanina J. Draughn, you are my mentor, my hero and my sister. Like you always say, "Sisters Forever."

To Boys Hope Girls Hope of Detroit: Without this program I would not have made it through high school. "There's no place like Hope!"

To my best friends, Rush L. Lockhart IV and Rosemary G. Kenrick; for all your support and for how much you encourage me in all that I do.

Also, thanks to my church families—Springhill Baptist Church and Metropolitan Baptist Church.

Give thanks in all circumstances, for this is
God's will for you in Christ Jesus.
—1 Thessalonians 5:18

Dedication

I dedicate this book to you because I love you so. Even though you left this world, I thought you ought to know.

I dedicate this book to you because you always told me yes. No matter what the circumstance you would say I always have success.

I dedicate this book to you to show you appreciation. For all of your hard work and struggles to me you are a "fighting temptation."

I dedicate this book to you because of your love and generosity, but most of all because you were my most special auntie.

Dedicated to: Elaine A. Davenport
November 9th, 1947 – March 5th, 2003
"Gone, but not forgotten"

Inside

my

Head

By Courtney E. Butts

Table of Contents

The Lord's Prayer...1
Introduction...3
Inside My Head..5

Part 1: Family
The One Who Left Me...9
What You Were to Me..10
Watch Me Now...11
In My Heart..12
Thank You..13
My Mother...14
Always Have My Love..16
Losing You...17
Look into My Eyes...18
Blood is Thicker..19
Josh Darnell, My Dad..20
My Family in Christ...21
My Hero...23

Part 2: Friends
Never Give Up...27
My Friend...28
Could I Ask for Better Friends?......................................30
Connected at the Heart..32

Part 3: Love
Lost in Love: Part I..37
One Moment of Your Time..39
Love at First Sight...41

If You Really Loved Me...43

If I Gave You...44

High School Love..45

Lost in Love: Part II...47

Part 4: A Friend in Need

Just Pray..51

Moving On..53

A Time to Say Goodbye...55

Never Leaving You...57

Part 5: Faith in God

Faith...63

Jesus is Watching...64

Dear God...66

Would He Take Me Back?..67

Take Away My Pain..68

Lord, You Saved Me...69

Another Chance at Life..71

Psalm...74

On a Mission for Christ...75

Take Control of My Life...78

Part 6: Reality

Who am I?...83

Left All Alone...85

I Cry...86

So Confused...87

The Brave One...88

Strong Will...89

Hear My Voice...90

CONTENTS

Crying Silent Tears...91

The Girl in the Mirror..92

What If..94

Destiny of Mine...95

Seen by All...96

In the Middle of it All..97

No One Understands..99

There's No Place Like Hope.............................100

The Real Me...103

The Person I Dream to Be: Strong, Black, and Beautiful...104

Survive..105

Struggle to Survive..106

They Said I Couldn't Do It...............................108

The Black Legacy..109

Understand Me...112

Just Sit and Listen...113

Diploma in My Hand..115

At Age Fourteen..117

My Legacy...119

Who I am...122

Closing Prayer...125

About the Author..127

The Lord's Prayer

Our Father in heaven,
Hallowed be Your name.
Your kingdom come.
Your will be done
On earth as it is in heaven.
Give us this day our daily bread.
And forgive us our debts,
As we forgive our debtors.
And do not lead us into temptation,
But deliver us from the evil one.
For Yours is the kingdom and the power
and the glory forever.
Amen.

—Matthew 6:9b-13

Introduction

This book started as a poetry assignment at Mumford High School in Mrs. Seabron's 9th grade English class. It was April and I had almost completed my freshman year. We were studying *Romeo and Juliet* and just as Shakespeare did, we had to write a sonnet. My sonnet was entitled "The one who left me" dedicated to my aunt who had died a month earlier. I decided to write a book and dedicate it to her. As I grew older, writing became more natural to me and I could write a poem about anything. This book tells the story of my life and my four years of high school—the up and downs, friendships, my spiritual life, my relationships and me finding myself. I love to leave the readers thinking after they have heard my poetry. After reading this book, I'm sure you will feel like in some way you know me or can relate to me.

The title of this book, "Inside My Head," came to me out of nowhere, yet it does state what I want my readers to know. In these past four years so much has passed through my mind, people have walked in and out of my life, and my self-esteem has changed. I am not the person I was when I began writing this book. I hope that you will be able to grow with me in this book, not from month to month or year to year, but from lost to saved.

God Bless You,
Courtney E. Butts

Inside My Head
Inspired by Shanina J. Draughn
February 2005

So many things bottled up inside of me,
So many things in this world that confuse me.
So many things I wish I could change,
Nobody knows my dreams—only my name.
I don't know at times who I want to be,
I don't know if I want to run away or just write poetry.
So many people try to help me and choose my path,
But the decision I make is the one that will last.
I pray to God every night, down on bended knee.
I need some guidance or just someone to listen to me.
I know this may sound funny, but I feel like I've hit rock
     bottom,
Like I'm in a room with no way out.
I can see people in front of me, but I can't speak to them.
I can only hear their voices but they can't hear me.
I'm trying to live right by just being me.
Everybody needs someone to talk with or just someone to
     love.
I wish I could float away to the Heavens above.
I love my life but I feel like I'm turning in circles.
Like every door or person I've seen before,
They're looking at me like I'm someone they adore.
But that's just a front because no one is real these days.
So many people question my clothes and my ways.
Did I choose this life for myself or did God plan it for me?
So many people are telling me 1-4-3,
But I can't believe it's the truth because it sounds like a lie.
At night all I do is cry while sitting on my bed,

While all the struggles of life float
Inside my head.

"Success is to be measured not so much by the position
that one has reached in life as by the obstacles which he
has overcome."

—Booker T. Washington

PART 1

Family

"Beloved, let us love one another, for love is of God;
and everyone who loves is born of God and knows
God. He who does not love does not know God, for
God is love."
—1 John 4:7-8, NKJV

The One Who Left Me

Dedicated to my aunt, Elaine A. Davenport
April 2003

A few months ago when you left me,
This was something I couldn't believe.
Even though I was young, I could now see,
You'll miss the many things I'll achieve.
When I was young, you taught me how to read,
Bandaged my cuts, if they had bled.
Because of you in my life I'll succeed,
You could fix anything as I already said.
It makes no sense to keep dreading the past,
In a few years, I'll be graduating at the top of my class,
Nowhere near last.
Truth be told I'm not exaggerating.
I hope you're enjoying life in your new place,
Wait for me again one day; I'll see your face.

"Jesus said to her, 'I am the resurrection and the life.
He who believes in me will live, even though he dies;
and whoever lives and believes in me will never die.
Do you believe this?'"
—John 11: 25-26

What You Were to Me

Dedicated to my aunt, Elaine A. Davenport
March 2003

You were my everything; you filled my heart with joy. You were the auntie that bought the best toys. You were there to listen when no one else was around. You were the voice that had a comforting sound. You were more to me than these simple words can explain. You were the one that showed me life could be a joyful game. You were there for me all the days of my life until I was fourteen years of age. To me, you were like a bird trapped in a cage. You are the one who has broken through those bars that held you back. I'm not sad that you left me, just a little hurt. I'll always remember what you wore—even your favorite shirt. I'm not going to say goodbye, I'm just going to say, "Until then... Until I meet you at the gates of Heaven. I didn't know it when you left, but you were a lot of things. But most important to me, you were my closet auntie."

Watch Me Now . . .

Dedicated to my aunt, Elaine A. Davenport
April 2003

Watch me now as I grow; I really want you to know.

Stay with me as angel by my side.

Lead me through life and be my guide.

Watch me now as I grow; I really want you to know.

A young child I may be; I know you left this world to be
free.

Watch me now as I grow; I really want you to know.

I may be hurt, but you made me strong;

I will think of you all day long.

Watch me now and walk with me...

I am still your little baby girl, you see.

I used to wish that you'd come back, but you're in a

better place and you would never do that.

I'll be fine; don't worry Auntie,

God sent me a healer that I did need.

You didn't have any children of your own,

but you acted as if we were all living in your home.

This is not a time to be sad, rather a time to be glad,

because you're in a better place.

Wait for me and forget me not.

Up there in Heaven, please save me a spot.

I will end this poem just as it began...

Watch me now as I grow; I really want you to know.

Because of all your love and generosity,

I dedicate this poem to my most special auntie.

"For this God is our God for ever and ever; he will be
our guide even to the end."   —Psalm 48:14

In My Heart

Dedicated to my aunt, Elaine A. Davenport
November 2003

When I close my eyes
To go to sleep,
Many memories of you will I keep
In my heart like you were always here.
You are my guardian angel and
I know that you are near.
I don't think you're really dead
Because your spirit is not gone.
An eternity in Heaven, you will live on.

Thank You

Dedicated to my mom, Janet C. Baxter
January 2004

So many words to describe the way I feel.
So many times when I didn't think I could make it, but
   I did.
So many questions that you answered for me.
So many people in my life but you're my everything.
So many decisions to help improve my life.
So many dangers like conviction or a stab from a knife.
So many things that I can't get through.
This is much easier Mom, because of you.

My Mother

Dedicated to my mom, Janet C. Baxter
April 2004

You're the first voice I hear in the morning, and the
     last smile I see at night.
You're the one who made everything better
     when I wasn't feeling alright.
You are my everything even when we don't get along,
I'm blessed to have a mother who lets me stay in her
     home
—After all my mistakes and my screw-ups,
You always turned to me and said: "Courtney keep
     your head up."
For as long as I can remember, it's been me,
     my sister and you.
I always follow you trying to do what you do.
No one can compare or replace a mother's love
I love you from the bottom of my heart
     to the Heavens above.
Things aren't the same like they used to be,
Because I've grown up into a young lady.
Temptations are around me,
     but you taught me to be strong.
You still love me even when I do wrong.
I want you to accept me and the changes in my life,
Because I respect yours
     even though they're not always nice.
No one can compare or even come close,
This one is to my mother the one I love the most.
I'm sad, I'm crying, I have many fears.

Family

I used to sit on your lap
   while you wiped away my tears.
I love all my family from one to another,
But the light of my life that would be:
My Mother.

They replied, "Believe in the Lord Jesus, and you will
be saved—you and your household."

                                   —Acts 16:31

Always Have my Love

Dedicated to my mom, Janet C. Baxter

July 2004

Things may not be exactly the way they should be,
But I still love you like I know you love me.
The decisions you make I do question,
As I stand here today, I have to make a confession.
I'm scared to leave you; you're my everything,
You mean the world to me, in my life so much joy do you
 bring.
I'm worried about life and I really feel stressed
But I know the Lord will guide me because I'm truly
 blessed.
Let me try, please give me another chance,
As I look at this situation, I take a second glance.
I see this situation as you giving up on me,
Why Mommy, the reason I just can't see.
I've developed a lifestyle that will quickly change,
My friends are left puzzled with questions unexplained.
I didn't agree with your decision but I can't complain,
No matter what happens, I'll always treat you the same.
Remember this Mom I will always be your child,
And when I think of you, I will always smile.
From the bottom of my heart to the Heavens above,
No matter what, you will *always have my love.*

Losing You

Dedicated to my mom, Janet C. Baxter
July 2004

I am your last child, your youngest baby girl.
For as long as I can remember, you've been my whole
world.
While I was growing up all I had was you.
Not even a father to look up to.
As I grew older the good times remained,
But I knew I was in trouble when you said my full
name.
We made it through elementary and all the way
through eighth grade.
If I would have known life would be this tough, in your
arms I would have stayed.
Now I'm in high school, we've started to drift apart.
In my life you don't play such an important part.
I don't know why you made this decision to give up on
me, but maybe living with you is not my destiny.
If it's something I did, please let me take it back.
I apologize anyways as a matter of fact.
If it's something I said, I'm sorry I swear.
Even if I was right, I don't even care.
The thought of me leaving brings tears to my eyes.
I'll tell you everything all the secrets and lies.
Can I have one more chance to be your child?
I'm really going to miss your voice and your smile.
Sometimes we do things we don't want to do,
But I just can't bear the fact that I'm *losing you.*

Look Into My Eyes

Dedicated to my mom, Janet C. Baxter
December 2004

Look into my eyes and see what I see,
A beautiful black woman starring back at me.
A beautiful black woman with a twinkle in her eye,
A beautiful black woman who I know would never lie.
Look into my eyes and see what I see,
A beautiful black woman starring back at me.
A beautiful black woman who really knows me,
She knows my name and my personality.
She knows my ways and how I like to joke around,
She knows I was lost and searching, but now I am
    found.
She knows I'm shy, but I will change,
She knows that to her, I'll try not to complain.
I don't even have to mention your name,
I said beautiful woman so it's all the same.
Look into my eyes see what I see,
A beautiful black woman starring back at me.
But really look into my eyes and see what I see,
A beautiful black queen smiling back at me.

Blood is Thicker

Dedicated to my family

December 2004

My family is loving and they always stay true,
My family is protective to the old and the new.
My family is unique...some big, some small.
My family is strong, we will never fall.
My grandma is the back that holds us all together;
She's the heart and soul of our family and there is no
better.
My family is my own and I love them to death,
With all of my heart; to my very last breath.
My family is always quick to help someone who is feeling
blue,
And always quick to say "I love you"
My family is made up of grandparents, cousins, and
brothers,
We also have a strong line of wonderful, sister,
fathers and mothers.
My family is middle class but our love of life is richer,
At the end of the day, the blood of love is thicker.

"Only be careful, and watch yourselves closely so that you
do not forget the things your eyes have seen or let them
slip from your heart as long as you live. Teach them to your
children and their children after them."

—Deuteronomy 4:9

Josh Darnell, My Dad

Dedicated to Josh D. Mobley
December 2004

I don't remember every single moment we shared,
I don't remember if you were violent or even if you did
    swear.
I don't remember laughing with you on Christmas Day,
I don't remember my favorite game that we used to play.
I don't remember every single picture that we took,
But I do remember everyone always said I had your looks.
I don't remember how old you were when I was born,
I don't remember if you prefer fries or creamed corn.
I don't remember us eating watermelon on the Fourth of
    July,
I don't remember a lot, I have no clue why.
I don't remember every smile, or every cry we had.
But I thank God that you're my Dad.
I don't remember the past, but Dad I'll forget you never,
One thing I'll always remember is I'm going to love you
forever.

"Honor your father and mother. Then you will live a long,
full life in the land the LORD your God is giving you."
—Exodus 20:12

My Family in Christ

Dedicated to Springhill Baptist Church
July 2006

I joined you all alone,
No family with me and I was unknown.
December was month, 04 was the year,
Walking in this place I felt that Christ was near.
I sat in the church with braids in my hair,
T-shirt and jeans because I didn't really care.
But that's a lie because Lord, I know I needed You,
Why else would I want to join a fellowship that only
    praises You?
I was shy at first and I would always keep silent.
I would pray and want my answers instantly,
I said, "God, why is all this happening to me?"
Just sitting in the church I didn't think I could change
    or even try,
But I knew something had to be done because at night
    all I would do is cry.
I didn't really know what to do so I ignored the past,
And before I knew it, a breakthrough came at last.
Out of they city and on the bus,
Loyal servants of God were all of us.
World Changers Mission Trip 2005,
For once in my life I felt like I was alive.
June twenty-third was the day,
A time had been called for all the youth to pray.
With youth workers in front of us, I had fear in my
    eyes,
Out poured my regrets and all of my lies.

I went to Shanina, someone I could trust,
I said my life has to change and that is a must.
I finally started to feel my connection with Christ,
I felt like I had just started a new life.
The more I opened my eyes, the more I started to see,
That I had a family right before me.
A family that loves me and loves Jesus Christ,
My baptism was significant even though it was done
    twice.
In church, I'm livelier and people are starting to know
    me,
I finally had a personality to go along with the face they
    see.
At Springhill Baptist Church, "We're building lives by
    the book,"
I feel like a fish because I got hooked on Christ,
Thank you, God, for saving my life.
At first, I thought I had no family and I was all alone,
But we're all family, and I thank God for this church
    home.
Us kids always say "I C U" Which means "I see you
    Christ."
This slogan was created way back when,
Our question to the world is
Can you see Him?

My Hero
Dedicated to Shanina J. Draughn
June 2006

From the moment I met you,
I never knew that we could grow so close.
I never thought you were the one I would look up to the
    most.
You love me and care for me just like a best friend would
    do.
And you support me and pray for me like a sister would do.
The reason why we're so close is that we're connected in
    Christ,
You were there for me the day I said, "Lord, take my life."
I used to think a hero could only be somebody famous on
    T.V.,
But you know what's funny? You're famous in my heart,
I'm blessed because with you a relationship I did start.
In good times and bad times, you always encourage me to
    pray,
And you never questioned me about my thoughts or my
    ways.
Sometimes I don't understand what you say or do,
But I try to understand because I have so much respect for
    you.
I know sometimes you think of me as just another child,
But in the end I can always make you laugh and smile.
In life, I'll find struggles no matter where I go,
And to me you'll always be a best friend, sister and my
    hero.

"Though I have fallen, I will rise. Though I sit in darkness, the Lord will be my light."

—Micah 7:8b

PART 2

Friends

"Don't walk in front of me, I may not follow.
Don't walk behind me, I may not lead.
Just walk beside me and be my friend."
—Albert Camus

Never Give Up

Dedicated to Lydia A. Young
March 2004

People say there's no point trying it's through,
Everybody says I should give up on you.

People say that our friendship just won't make it,
But I see this as a risk and yes I'm going to take it.

People say stop causing myself all this pain,
Together as friends we will remain.

People say together us two just don't belong,
I know our friendship is right but "they" say it's wrong.

People say that you make me have to lie,
But I love you with all my heart and I will never say
     goodbye.

People say that only want what's best for me,
But that's you and "they" just can't see.

People say they only do it because they care,
You're one of a kind and no one can compare.

People say that I am just out of luck,
But on you I will *never give up*

My Friend

Dedicated to Danielle D. Greer
March 2004

We got off to a bad start,
but now we're like sisters; we're never apart.
When people look for you, all they have to do is find me.
At first we hated each other, but soccer brought us
together, you see.
We've been through a lot, and many secrets have been
shared,
When you let me cry on your shoulder, I really know you
cared.
When I'm upset I look for you to ease my pain and calm
me down,
I thank the Lord for this extra special friend I've found.
When you see a frown on me, you quickly turn it around.
When I cry you make me laugh.
I brought you to my house and you called it your second
home,
You have a friend like me and you'll never be alone.
We've only known each other for one year
but we already have a past,
Until the days when I grow old, I know our friendship will
last.
You're my cousin, my sister, but most of all you're my
friend.
I know you'll always be by my side to help me out if you
can.
Remember those days in the summer of 2003,
When you were at my house every day after three?

Yeah those times were fun and there are many more to
    come,
Every time I ate something, you always wanted some.
But all jokes aside I want to speak from my heart,
I thank God for making you become a part.
It was a little blurry at first but now it's all clear,
I blessed to have a friend like Danielle Greer.

"Carry each other's burdens,
and in this way you will fulfill the law of Christ."
—Galatians 6:2

Could I Ask for Better Friends?

Dedicated to: Rosemary Kenrick, Arielle Leak,
Hillary Rutan, Leah Haapala
June 2006

You laugh with me,
You go to church with me,
You run with me,
And you pray with me.

Four different friends,
With four different names,
But who all love me
Even though things sometimes change.

You met me one minute and we were joking around
the next,
We're so much alike, yet different, and our friendship
is complex.
We're never separated, we're always together.
You are my best friend and there is no one better.

You comfort me when I'm not feeling the best,
And you understand that we're both loved, cared for
and blessed.
You connected with me in a whole different way,
You'll stop with me any minute when I need to pray,

You'll be there to the very end of all time,
You're the one I always keep on my mind.
You're the one that always encourages me and keeps

me cool
And you're the one I feel like I've known since pre-
school.

Connected at the Heart

Dedicated to Rosemary G. Kenrick

June 2006

It's funny how you sat across from me and I didn't
    recognize you.
At first, you blended in like every other girl
Who wore a plaid skirt and Birkenstock shoes.
But, in an instant it seemed like we became the best of
    friends,
And I intend to keep it this way until the very end.
Our friendship is unique; we're as different as day and
    night,
We argue about silly things because we both like being
    right.
But let me get down to the facts about you and me.
Let me jot down a couple notes about how much you mean
    to me.
I met you two years ago when I was struggling and lost,
Yet you still loved and cared for me and
    told me to turn towards the cross.
I think of you more like a sister than just my friend;
I'll be here to help you out if I can.
We're complete opposites when it comes to our stories,
    our futures and our past.
But, we both love Christ; that's why our friendship will last.
It seems like just yesterday we were relaxing and playing it
    cool.
Now we're in tears because it's our last day of school.
We sometimes fight but what good friends don't?
We sometimes forget to include one another,

Sometimes being too protective, acting like the other's
    mother.
All in all, one chapter of our life is closed.
Always and forever in my heart you will I hold.
Rosemary and Courtney: we're connected at the heart,
And we will be friends till death do us part.

"A real friend is one who walks in when the rest of the
world walks out."

                       —Unknown

PART 3

Love

"A new commandment I give to you: Love one another. As I have loved you, so you must love one another. By this all men will know that you are My disciples, if you have love for one another."

—John 13:34-35

Lost in Love
Part I
March 2004

It's like you have a curse on me; I can't think for myself,
It's like I work all day, and I give you all my wealth.
It's like I have a map, but I still can't find my way,
It's like we're on the phone, but I don't know what to say.
It's like you dumped me, but I still want to be with you,
It's like you saying you hate me, but I'm still saying "I love
    you."
It's like the feeling I have when we are not together,
It's like you were gone for a week, and it felt like forever.
It's like I have the money, but I don't want to pay the price,
It's like you're mean to me, but I still remained nice.
It's like I'm in the closet without any clothes,
It's like I'm on the street passing by all my friends and foes.
It's like I want to go out, but I have nothing to wear,
It's like I'm wishing I was with you, but all I can do is sit
    and stare.
It's like I can't speak, so I write you a note,
It's like being outside in the winter without a coat.
It's like I'm in the house, but it doesn't feel like my home,
It's like I'm with somebody, but I still feel alone.
It's like I want to eat something but I don't have an
    appetite,
It's like you're always wrong, but I still say your right.
It's like I forgot your gift on Valentine's Day,
It's like you wanting to leave, and me begging you to stay.
It's like I wake up in the morning and you're by my side,
It's like the day you dumped me, and I just broke down and

cried.

I was in love with you, and you were in love with another,
I was so in love with you,
I was willing to put you before my mother.
It's like we go together like Will and Jada Pickett Smith,
Our love is unbelievable, it seems like a myth.
It's like you're an angel, a princess, a goddess, or a dove,
It's like this because with you I'm just so *lost in love*.

One Moment of Your Time
March 2004

Excuse me; may I have one moment of your time?
Hello, how are you doing? Me, I'm doing just fine.
I don't know you yet, but I feel a connection,
I love your features and light skin complexion.
I want to learn a lil' more about your personality,
I have dreams of you at night, but I want to make it a
    reality.
I know I kept this a secret for a while,
But the truth is coming out because I love your smile.
Would you please give me a chance or the time of day?
If you listen to me, I bet I can persuade
    you to be with me and us to be together.
If others tell you I'm cheating, just say whatever.
When I speak to you, I speak from the heart,
You're extra special to me and you're extra smart.
Don't play with my emotions; I don't have times for games,
No matter what you wear, I will still treat you the same.
Can I have the honor of giving you a kiss?
I want many things but this is my number one wish.
Come on let's take a walk through the park walking hand-
    in-hand,
Also, let me tell you about my lifelong plans.
To me you're like no other,
    you're the one I would bring home to my mother.
Ok that's it, go home and think about this,
While you're not in my presence you'll truly be missed.
Before I leave, can I give you the number to my cell?
If you give me yours, no one will I tell.
338-8407 when we're talking I feel I could float up to
    heaven.
Twenty minutes later, after I walked you home,

I saw your digits pop up on my phone.
You said the same thing that I first said to you.
"May I have a moment of your time, to ask you how are
you?"

Love at first sight
April 2004

Do you believe in love at first sight?

I do.

From the very minute I saw you,

I knew I was in love with you.

I didn't know you but

I felt a special connection with you.

Wait let me slow down, let me tell you my name.

It's Courtney and trust me,

I'm not trying to run any game.

If you're not feeling me like that

As friends, I hope we will remain.

I'm so in love with you,

I forgot to ask you your name.

What is it?

It must be Angel because that's what you are to me.

If it cost everything I owned for us to be,

I'd give it up all instantly.

If I can't be rich with money,

I'll be rich with love.

You're like an angel that was sent to me

from the Heavens above.

I hope I'm not rushing you or putting any pressure on
you.

If I am, I'll slow down

I just can't believe this beauty that I've found

I've been searching for years and I've been

Through many painful break-ups and long nights full
of tears.

I'll know you'll never bring a tear to my eye
Except for the day you said you and I could be.
I couldn't even imagine you without me.
You and I we were destined to be.
My love for you is as simple as saying: 1-2-3.
You're like one-of-a-kind and I want you to be all mine.
You're on my mind all the time.
24 hours, 7 days a week.
When we're not together I feel kind of weak,
To you, at first, I was scared to speak.
Lost for words...speechless you might say,
I'll love you forever and always.
My love for you is something that I know is right.
Again I ask do you believe in
love at first sight?

If You Really Loved Me

May 2004

If you really loved me, you would have never walked away.

If you really loved me, you would listen to the words I say.

If you really loved me, you would understand my pain.

If you really loved me, you wouldn't have treated our love
like a game.

If you really loved me, you would walk on burning sand.

If you really loved me, you would find a way to hold my
hand.

If you really loved me, you would have asked me if I cared.

If you really loved me, my secrets you wouldn't have
shared.

If you really loved me, you'd buy me a simple red rose.

If you really loved me, you would have treated me better I
suppose.

If you really loved me, you would understand why we just
couldn't be.

If you really loved me, you would understand why love
wasn't meant for you and me.

"Above all. love each other deeply, because love covers
over a multitude of sins."

—I Peter 4:8

If I Gave You. . .

May 2004

If I gave you the chance, would you make the right
   choice?
If I gave you the time, would you let me hear your
   voice?
If I gave you my heart, would you give me your love?
If I gave you a bird, would you call it a dove?
If I gave you some helpful advice, would you take it?
If I tried out for the team, do you think I would make
   it?
If I gave you a complement that you didn't like,
Would you take it to the heart and hit me with all your
   might?
If I gave you an honest answer to questions that you
   asked,
Would you look at me differently as the time passed?
If I gave you my word and all of my trust,
Would you say I was a liar and call my feelings lust?
If I gave you the chance to play a different role,
Would you choose to play me and look into my soul?
If I gave you my body, would you abuse it?
If I gave you the key to my heart, would you ever lose
   it?
If I gave you nothing but discomfort and pain,
Would you toss me aside, forgetting my name?
If I gave you the choice of being with me,
Would you turn away or bend down on one knee?
If I gave you my love, and you didn't run,
Would you be honored if I called you "The One?"

✝

High School Love
September 2004

One day when I was lonely, I wished upon a star.
Then the next day in the mall, I saw you from afar.
I walked up to you real confident and smooth,
When I told you my intentions, I was happy that you
  approved.
I called you a while later to make some weekend plans.
And before that night was over
I had dreams of us walking hand-in-hand.
I finally had someone; you're my boy and I'm your girl,
I felt like you and I together shared our own special world.
You are so beautiful, that's why I always keep you near,
The thought of losing you is what I often feared.
Throughout the years in high school everybody knew,
That at all the parties I'd be walking in with you.
Remember that day March 16th of 02,
The first time I said that I was in love with you?
You call me your girl but I call you my partner in life,
One day in the future I hope to be your wife.
Last year in high school--what are we going to do?
Cause I have a scholarship and you have one too
I'm headed north and you're staying here,
Our relationship ending, that's what I fear.
We can work this out just like we did before,
As the days pass on I love you even more and more.
My mind says move on but my heart is stuck on you,
It's hard even to picture my life without you.
Come on we have to talk; we have to work this out.
What have all these years of our love been about?

Was it puppy love or was it real?

I know what I must do, bow down my head and kneel.

God will take care of it if we are truly meant to be together,

And if we're not, I'll forget you never.

Three more weeks have passed and I still don't know what
　　to do,

I am torn between going to a great college and spending
　　my life with you.

I got a full, four-year scholarship down in Tennessee,

So I've decided to move on and see where my life leads me.

You and I go together perfect just like a hand in a glove,

And I will always remember you as

My high school love.

Lost in Love
Part II
March 2005

I'm going to start this one the way I started the first,
It's like on me you've got some type of curse.
It's like with you, my heart is complete,
It's like you and I were destined to meet.
It's like you're a genie and you've just granted my wish,
It's like the very first time that we did kiss.
It's like the tingle I feel in my heart when you're around,
It's like my soul was lost, but now it is found.
It's like the smile on my face when our eyes met,
It's like standing at the altar and my hands start to sweat.
It's like the day I confessed my love to you
It's like I said I love you and you already knew.
It's like you can love my pain away,
It's like we went to the movies and you let me pay.
It's like I would do anything for you,
Jump in front of a moving car or take a bullet for you.
It's like to you, I would never tell a lie,
It's like on bended knee, for you, I would cry.
It's like I'm your Juliet, you're my Romeo,
It's like I got you in my arms, and I'll never let you go.
It's like we're not alike, but opposites attract,
It's like I don't live in the hood, but I'm still black.
It's like I play soccer, and you play softball,
It's like I'm writing poems, and you're shopping at the
    mall.
It's like you love me in a way I could never understand,
It's like you're scared, but I still hold your hand.

It's like the day you gave me a second chance,
It's like at me, you took a second glance.
It's like we broke up, and it broke my heart,
It's like when you left, so did a piece of my heart.
It's like living without a piece of me,
It's like me telling you constantly 1-4-3.
It's like we fought and I'm the only one it's harming,
It's like this is a fairy tale and you're my prince charming.
It's like I'm in a daze and don't know what to do,
It's like this because I'm so *lost in love* with you.

PART 4

A Friend In Need

"Greater love has no one than this, that he
lay down his life for his friends. You are
my friends if you do what I command."
—John 15:13-14

Just Pray

September 2004

Hello Alex, how are you doing today?
I'm not sure because I think I'm gay.

What do you mean; you were fine the other day?
I know but this girl was looking at me in a funny way

And so what, Alex this is not you.
I know Courtney please help me because I don't know
  what to do.

I don't know how but I'm going to help you some way,
One thing we can do is kneel down and pray.

Dear God,
I come to you today to be forgiven and to be guided
  because I've been mixed up with the wrong group
  and false information I've been provided.
Please Lord; lead me in the right way.
As a child of God I know I shouldn't be this way.
Adam and Eve were created for a reason.
Please God on me don't give up.
My mind is so confused it just might erupt.
God please forgive me and hold my hand.
In Jesus name I pray,
Amen.

God will hear your prayer and He'll do what He knows
  is best,

I hope so because this is bearing a lot of weight on my
    chest.

I'm so afraid, please guide me.
Don't worry Alex you can lean on me.

But I think I like a girl what should I do?
Just as I told you before, pray and the answer will
    come to you.

"But if you stay joined to me and my words remain in
you, you may ask any request you like, and it will be
granted."

—John 15:7, NLT

Moving On

September 2004

With my eyes I look around,
I saw on your face there was a frown.

I asked you if I could make you smile,
And you replied: "Not for a while."

Tell me your story and I will listen,
This happened on a day that you did not witness.
What happened Alex? Was it bad?
Look at my face, don't I look sad?

My mom left me; I don't know where she's at,
She's probably never coming back

Don't worry, Alex she loves you, now let me tell you
    what you should do.
Pray to God, down on bended knee and if you're still
    struggling come back to me.

I love you Courtney,
And you know I love you too.

I wish that I could come home with you,
Come on you can, I'll never leave you.
I'll help you out and make sure you achieve.

I don't know why she left but I miss her so,
Did she ever love me, how will I ever know?

I will always remember her and her gift of song,
Come on Alex; let's go because we're *moving on.*

"Faith comes from hearing the message, and the message is heard through the word of Christ."

—Romans 10:17

A Time to Say Goodbye

September 2004

Come on Alex, you've got to get out of bed,
I just can't do it; did you hear what I said?

This is your last chance to say your final goodbye,
I won't even be able to look her in the eye.

Your mother would want you to be there on this day
Even if you don't get up and pray

Okay, I'll do it, but only if you're with me,
I have to say something in her memory.

We arrive at the church. Alex was nervous as ever,
Come on she'll be resting in eternity forever.

Take my hand; let's walk slow.
It's my time, respect we must show.

I saw her face, her eyes, and hair,
This pain I just cannot bear.

Wait Courtney, don't come I need to do this alone,
Let me say goodbye to my mother as she makes her journey home.

Alex walked up to the coffin her hand on her chest,
And the only thing she said was:
"Mother, enjoy your rest."

You did it I heard you; you are really brave,
I don't know if I can watch my mother being put in her
grave.

At the funeral, I rose and had this to say:
No longer shall you hurt, not for a single day.
No longer will you live in this cruel unsafe world,
All you left behind was your little baby girl.
No more pain and no more sorrow,
I'll talk to you when I pray to God tomorrow.

Even though I was scared to look in my mother's eye,
This prayer I dedicate to my mother, because it's
A time to say goodbye.

Never Leave You
September 2004

Tonight is the night.
It's your big day.

I know you can't believe it.
Does my hair look right this way?

Yes it's beautiful, don't worry about it,
Oh my goodness Courtney, my shoes don't fit.

Calm down Alex, those are mine,
Relax, you have plenty of time.

Four hours later, I heard the ring of the bell.
Alex was getting nervous, I could already tell.

Let's go downstairs our dates have arrived.
Wait Courtney, because without you, I wouldn't have
    survived.

I just have to say, thank you for helping me cope, and
    always giving me advice and a little bit of hope.

It was nothing, really, just forget it.
No, now it's your time to listen, so go ahead and sit.

Since freshman year you've been there to guide
    and protect, and you always helped me.
Even when I thought that I was out of luck
    you turned to me and said:

"Alex, on you I'll never give up."

Ok I understand.

No, let me continue because without you
   I would not have made it through.
This is important to me because you saved my life.
I passed all the tests despite the hatred and strife.
I think you're my guardian angel
   because you always watch me so close.
You're all that I have, and I love you the most.

Thank you Courtney, for all of these things;
But I thank you most for being a friend to me.

All of my tears came at once
I couldn't stop crying because I love you so much.

Come here Alex let me give you a kiss
After tonight, you I'll truly miss

No you won't

It's the end of this journey, but a new one will begin,
Just like you, I'm headed to U of M.

Don't cry, Courtney. We have to enjoy this night,
My mother is probably above like an angel in flight.

My make-up is ruined and yours is too.

A Friend in Need

Alex I got your back,
And I got yours too.

PART 5

Faith in God

"You are the salt of the earth; but if the salt loses its saltiness, how can it be made salty again? It is no longer good for anything, except to be thrown out and trampled by men. You are the light of the world."
—Matthew 5:13-14a

Faith

February 2000

Faith.
What is faith? Is faith me? Is faith you?
Is faith the things we are supposed to do?
I've heard of people by the name of faith,
Does that mean they have faith or need faith?
Again, I ask what is faith?

"Now Faith is being sure of what we hope for
and certain of what we do not see."　—Hebrews 11:1

Jesus Is Watching

August 2004

When you wake up in the morning, give Him thanks.

A higher position in His eyes you will rank.

As your day goes on, He follows you around,

A new group of friends you have found.

They don't worship or even pray,

As a child of God, what do you say?

Nothing because you're scared,

To admit that you honor His name.

But think,

What would you do if Jesus were right here with you?

Would you change your decision or still do what you do?

Would you spread the word of God to the ones who don't
believe?

Or, would you ignore it and brush it off like dirt on your
sleeve?

Being a child of God is difficult these days,

Because many have drifted away from His words and His
ways.

But, God singled you out to bring others back.

Look it up in the good book for the verse to be exact.

Remember that day a bullet hit your chest?

But you're walking again because you're truly blessed.

Satan is out recruiting—getting in peoples' minds,

If he confronts you, point to your heart and say, "Jesus is
in mine."

Some people only think of God when there is a death,

But no matter the circumstance,

He'll be with you to your last breath.

He knows what you've thought, He knows what you've

said.

But He'll forgive you if you just bow your head.

Don't think, "What do I want to do?"

Think, "What would Jesus do?"

Does He want me to sit here and just play a game,

Or go out and glorify His name?

At the end of the day when you are back at home,

Because you have Jesus on your side, you will never be
alone.

Before you crawl into your bed and end the day,

Bend down and don't forget to pray.

Out of your mouth these words you must say,

"Thank you Lord for another day."

"For the eyes of the Lord are on the righteous and his ears
are attentive to their prayer..."

—I Peter 3:12a

Dear God

December 2004

Dear God,

It's me again Courtney—better known as the star.

When I look up to the Heavens, You seem so far.

But I know You're right here in my heart

Because You're a part of me.

God, I'm searching for my purpose and my true
   identity.

Lord, I have so many questions that I feel are left
   unexplained.

Is it in my destiny to have money and fame?

I'm just living in this world trying to make it,

But there are so many tragedies I just can't take it.

Lord, please keep my mother with me

Because without her, there is no me.

Watch out for my friends, especially Rosemary,
   Hillary, and Leah.

I don't know Your plans or what's going to happen
   next.

God, I may not be the strongest, but I'll survive,

I'm blessed that another day I'm alive.

I'm blessed to be here Lord, thank you.

God, I will forever love You.

Don't worry, I'll be back again,

In Jesus' name I pray,

Amen.

"Before they call I will answer; while they are still
speaking I will hear."
—Isaiah 65:24

Would He Take Me Back?

January 2005

If Jesus came back and walked on this earth,
Would I be satisfied with my life or want to restart it from
    birth?
If Jesus came back and wanted to talk to me,
Would I make up stories of myself like it was my reality?
If Jesus came back, could we be the best of friends?
Could I talk to Him without questioning His plan?
If Jesus came back, would I continue to pray?
Or would I just be living my life from day to day?
If Jesus came back, would I recognize Him?
Would he be tall and round, or skinny and slim?
If Jesus came back, would I know what to say?
Would I say: "Thank You for life," or just look away?
If Jesus came back, would my friendships remain?
Or would they turn away and deny my name?
If Jesus came back, the one who died for me...
Would I bend down on one knee, repent for my sins,
Beg for forgiveness, and say I'm sorry?
If Jesus came back, could I look Him in the eye?
Or would I put my head down like I was about to tell a lie?
If Jesus came back and had this to say:
"All who follow me, follow me again today"
Would God look down on me because I'm this way?
Would I be accepted in God's kingdom if I died today?

"Before I formed you in the womb I knew you, before you
were born I set you apart; I appointed you as a prophet to
the nations."   —Jeremiah 1:5

Take Away My Pain

Inspired by Shanina J. Draughn
January 2005

I did this to myself; I brought all the pain,
I brought back the tears and all the hurtful names.
But I'm older and wiser and I need to forget the past,
When I question myself, I should turn to the Lord and ask,
Why am I so concerned about things I can't control?
Why am I still carrying this burden so close to my soul?
Please God, help me, and I'll try not to complain.
All I need for You to do is
Take away my pain.

"I have told you these things, so that in me you may have
peace. In this world you will have trouble.
But take heart! I have overcome the world.'"

          —John 16:33

Lord, You Saved Me
Dedicated to Larissa & Lajoyclynn Powell
March 2005

I never knew how much I loved my life until I almost
    lost it.
I woke up on Saturday morning with not a care in my
    mind.
Got up, ate breakfast, and started on my way.
I never knew the circumstances that I would encounter
    on this day.
I arrived at class very early but some of my friends
    were already there,
We laughed at old times and complimented each
    other's hair.
Class had started and all I could think about was the
    end,
But at the end of the day I wish it wouldn't have began.
Leaving class at exactly a quarter to one with some
    loved ones with me.
I was destined to get home to watch some T.V.
I started off heading north on Cass toward the
    expressway,
Now that I know the result, I thank Jesus for that day.
I got onto the Lodge and merged to the left, I tried it
    again and I lost my breath.
Boom, a quick hit to my left side, the car went spinning
    and I almost cried.
Not one, two, three, but four times did we hit that wall.
Airbags deployed on both sides, again I almost cried.
We crawled out the car and my best friend fell to the

ground,
I searched and searched but my cell phone was no
    where to be found.
Back in the car, Peaches searched and found it under
    the seat.
I called my mother and said, "Please help me because I
    totaled your car;"
Sitting on the highway everything seemed so far.
Long story short, the Lord saved me.
Some say it was the seatbelts but my God saved me.
On February 12th we survived; it was God's plan for us
    to stay alive.

"Trust in the Lord with all your heart and lean not on your
own understanding; in all your ways acknowledge him, and
he will make your paths straight."

—Proverbs 3:5-6

Another Chance at Life

Springhill Baptist Church Youth Group
July 2005

I stood there knowing that I wasn't happy with my life,
Knowing that there was a way for me to see the light.
Those people stood before me, because they love and
they care.
As the tears rolled down my cheeks I knew this pain I
couldn't bear.
I ran to the arms of someone that I could trust,
With so many feelings of hatred and lust.
I didn't say a word, you already knew,
What was troubling my heart and what I had been
through.
I thank you for being the hands to hold, arms to hug,
ears to listen and heart to love.
Everything happens for a reason and I believe God
sent you to me from above.

I thought that this would make me happy.
But in reality I was a child, scared straight, running
away from my fears.
Looking for a way out after two long years.
The longest two years of my very short life.
I don't know how I survived when I walked away from
Christ.

I was at the lowest point, "rock bottom" you might say.
God loved me so much that again He showed me the
way.
I don't think I was really gone, just blinded by the

light…blinded by fame,
So many people scream out my name.
Like they're fans of me and they admire what I do.
I was living my life like "Monkey see, monkey do".

But that's not me; I'm always ahead of the crowd.
Doing big things and making my mom proud.
I stood there in that dark tunnel knowing what was
    right,
Yet as the time passed, I kept walking away from the
    light.

But God has a plan that was much different than mine.
I could feel the love of God like it was going through
    my spine.
I often think to myself "What is my greatest fear?"
That man putting his hands on me or was it my vision
    of Christ, which isn't clear.
I don't know why, but something came over me that
    day
And that voice inside my head said "Courtney, why are
    you this way?"

Standing there alone looking at all of my peers,
Wondering what I had missed out on those two long
    years.
Nothing in life is easy and this is one task that will be
    hard.
I think I'm going to fail like in school when I get a D,
But "I can do all things with Christ who strengthens
    me."
I'm ready to recommit my life to the one that died for

me.

The one who knew my plan before I was even
    conceived.

When I think about this it seems like a dream,

Of a child who wanted to cry out and scream.

I'm a child of God and if He spoke to me today,

"I want you to spread My Word," is what He would say.

I have the love of God that I want to share with others.

So in Christ I can have more sisters and brothers.

It's my time now to check into the game,

Step up to the plate or move into the fast lane.

I'm done sitting on the bench with people who don't
    believe,

They just brush you off like its dirt on their sleeve.

God forgive me, for losing my faith in You

And turning away when I most needed You.

At the end of my days, before I shed my very last tear

"Well done good and faithful servant" is what I want to
    hear.

"I can do all things with Christ who strengthens me."

                         —Philippians 4:13, NKJV

Psalm

Inspired by Ms. Elek, Marian High School
October 2005

Dear God,

Before I took my earthly form, You knew my whole
    plan.
You loved and cared for me.
I was born into a world of sin, and tempted by the
    darkest valley of evil.
I followed You and I did my best to live by Your Word.

I come to You on bended knee with a heart full of
    regret.
Praising You, worshiping You,
I fear no one but You.
I am here to do Your work as Your servant.

As said in Romans 12:1-2; "Therefore, I urge you
    brothers, in full view of God's mercy, to offer Your
    bodies as living sacrifices, holy and pleasing to
    God—this is your spiritual act of worship. Do not be
    conformed to the pattern of this world, but be trans-
    formed by the renewing of your mind. Then you will
    be able to test and approve what God's will is—his
    good, pleasing, and perfect will." [1]

I beg of You now for forgiveness and praise.
I will always love You and worship Your name.
Until my task is completed,
I will live in Thy Father's kingdom forever.
Amen.

[1] New International Version

On A Mission for Christ

Dedicated to Mallory Draughn
Springhill Baptist Church Youth Ministry
January 2006

Without God, I would have nothing at all.
Without God in my life, I would continuously fall.

I was raised in the church, but I didn't really believe.
I was just on the pew taking up space.
But, because of God, I was saved by grace.
Fourteen-year-old freshman in high school searching
    for my "clique;"
From jocks to seniors which one would I pick?

Satan walked in to my life, but I didn't even recognize
    him.
For two long years, I called him my best friend.
At first, I didn't realize who really stood before me,
But I quickly found myself alone on bended knee.

I found myself in worship again because someone
    loved me.
Many sleepless nights I had to face.
Deep into the night, all I could do was pace—and
    wonder to myself,
Why does God love me?
I'm not worthy of a Savior as great as He.

It was like so many messages were being sent to me.
Every billboard and poster had something for me.
Philippians 4:13 reads: "I can do all things with Christ

who strengthens me."

I heard the Word and confessed my faith.
I was baptized in the Spirit and began a new race.

My life is like a journey, and I'm running to the end.
Being baptized, to me, was like a new life had begun.
Many obstacles of this cruel world try to stop me,
But I'm a follower of God and no one can break me.

I don't know how long I'm going to be here with the
    ability to spread the Word.
Every cry from the sick and hungry is to be heard.
The cross I wear on my chest means not one thing
If I don't spread the Gospel to the ones who don't
    believe.

Forgive me, O Lord. Yes, I've committed a sin.
    Fighting without You is a battle I cannot win. Help
    me, Jesus, to live more like You and never again
    stray away from You. Lord, I love and adore You
    and I do all I can, as your loyal servant, I will do
    Your plan. In Jesus' name, I pray. Amen.

No one can compare to You.
I have nothing, nothing at all without You.
You are not only my Father, but also my very best
    friend;
You are the only One I can call on again and again.

So many material things have blinded me:
Unfaithful friends and the greed of money.

Only the things you do for Christ will last.
This is 2006 and I've left all my baggage in the past.

If you ask who I am, I'll say, a member of God's team.
I'm for the One who loves me daily and died for me.
To sum this all up, I thought I'd lost my life,
But because I'm alive, *I'm on a mission for Christ.*

"While there's life, there's hope."
                                        —Terence [Publius Terentuis Afer]

Take Control of My Life

June 2006

I knelt down at the altar for a chance to confess, to
say that I am grateful and that I am truly blessed.
Never did I think this would be a breakthrough for
me. Constantly I cried out to the Lord, "I'm ashamed
and sorry." Lord, I know You're by my side when I
bend down on my knees. Lord, I know You guide me in
the path, which directs me away from the rapists and
thieves. I look at my life going so many ways and I try
to understand Your will and Your plan. Lord, thank
You for Your mercy and Your grace. Even though I
can't see You, I still have the faith to believe in You
because, Lord, You are great...greater than any "best
friend" to walk into my life. You'll stick closer than a
brother, and for me, You made a sacrifice. An earthly
best friend will let me down, time after time, but with
Christ on my side, the love of God will always shine. I
know Your plans for my life are greater than my eyes
can see.

Dear most gracious and heavenly Father, I have
come to Thee with my head bowed and my heart fully
praying that You hear my plea. I need You and I love
You more than anything. Without You, I would have
nothing at all. Not even a reason to write or play ball.
Lord, on this 20th day of June, I surrender myself to
You. I'm done trying to live my life for me and not for
You. I come to You so sentimentally hoping that You'll
forgive. Thank You, Lord, for giving me the chance to
live. Thank You for blessing me; Your love is all I need.

Who else would stay on that cross for me and bleed?
No other Lord, because You're so mighty and great.
For, no longer in my life will I take my life for granted,
or the people that are in my face, because Lord, I know
You did especially place: Shanina and Rosemary and of
course Hill. I love you guys with all my heart. We have
a friendship that's bonding and we will never part.
Lord, I know these blessings are all because of You and
that's why I'm surrendering myself to You. In the name
of Jesus, thank you for creating this land, In Jesus'
name I pray, Amen.

As I walk away from this altar, with tears in my eyes,
Lord I leave behind old friends and all of my lies. I
take away *YOU*. You're in control of it all. I may just be
one person, but my voice isn't small. O God, You know
my heart, mind, and soul; and now unto You Lord, I
declare that You're in control.

"To you, O Lord, I lift up my soul; in you I trust, O my
God! Do not let me be put to shame, nor let my
enemies triumph over me."

—Psalm 25:1

PART 6

Reality

"'For I know the plans I have for you,' declares
the Lord, 'plans to prosper you and not to harm
you, plans to give you a hope and a future.'"
—Jeremiah 29:11

Who Am I?

March 2004

Who am I?
That's a good question.
My name is Courtney,
But that's not telling you anything really.
To me of course this sounds kind of silly.
I'm 15 years old but there's much more to me,
I have a unique personality.
I have dreams I want to make become a reality-
But constantly people question my sexuality.
I have many things to accomplish and goals to pursue,
People are constantly telling me "Courtney that's not the
real you."
I love myself and I love life and I want to make it right.
I may not have seen everything, but I feel like I've "Seen
the light."
I'd give up everything I own to go back in time,
I wish I had a remote so I could just push rewind.
But I can't, it's over; time to make some changes now,
I need some guidance—someone to show me how.
Who am I? Is what I'm trying to discover,
The old Courtney Butts is who I'm trying to recover.
Who am I, a child who's lost?
Despite all that, I'm still a "06" Boss.
I have plans to go far, but first, I have to figure out who I
am.
I want to respect my elders and always say "Yes Ma'am."
I used to know, but I don't anymore;
I don't even wear the same type of clothes that I wore.
Who am I? Is the question, right now I just need to be

alone,
Because *who I am* still remains unknown.

"If I have lost confidence in myself, I have the world
against me."   —Ralph Waldo Emerson

Left All Alone
June 2003

It seems like you were here one day and gone the next,
I could be referring to Danielle or speaking of Flexx.
It doesn't matter who this poem is about,
You hurt me so bad that I scream and shout.
Why did you walk into my life, if you knew
You were going to walk away?
This is not a game; timeout, don't call the next play.
What more can I say? Trust me, it's a lot.
In my heart, I made you a spot.
I trust you with everything; in this friendship I give it
    my all,
You are those strong hands that pick me up when I fall.
You said you would never leave me, but now I know
    you lied,
I swear to God no more secrets will I hide.
You don't tell me everything and that's ok,
But with you I'll be open in each and every way.
When you left me it was like a piece of my soul,
Only when you come again I will be whole.
I want to ask you one question: Why did you leave me
    alone?
As quickly as it started, I will end this poem.

"The Lord is with me; I will not be afraid."
—Psalm 118:6a

I Cry

July 2003

At night I cry
So many tears do I shed,
Dreadful thoughts and memories
Fill my head.

I don't have anyone to talk to
No one at all to care,
No one at all to listen
This pain I cannot bear.
I pray to God
Down on bended knee
When will my time come,
For the Lord to get me?

At night I cry
So many tear do I shed
Dreadful thoughts and memories
Fill my head.

"Yet I am always with you; you hold me by my right
hand." —Psalm 73:23

So Confused

October 2003

So lonely and confused, mistreated and misused.
So lost and one-sided, scared and open minded.
So sorry and forgetful, jealous and resentful.
So senseless and afraid, hurt and betrayed.
So shy and mean, regretful and unseen.
So anonymous and quiet, patient and unsighted.
So lonely. . . .

and confused.

The Brave One

December 2003

I used to be scared, young and afraid,
But I've grown older and my dues have been paid.
I have to be brave because younger ones look up to me,
They watch my every move and learn nothing in life is free.
I used to be scared to see loved ones lying in their sick bed,
Now I can walk proudly and hold up my head.
I used to be scared of death,
And the thought of taking my last breath.
But your body is just an earthly shell.
Your soul will live on in either
Heaven or Hell.

Strong Will

Dedicated to: Janet C. Baxter

October 2003

I remember that you always taught me to be strong.

As a young child, I had to learn right from wrong.

I look nothing like you,

All my looks come from my Dad,

But you're the one, who was there

At night to tuck me in bed.

You taught me not to be weak,

And how to be strong,

You always told me how you loved me, and

That I can do anything if I just believe.

You told me I was an angel

And one day I would be a "star."

You made me strong, so I

Know my plans will take me far.

I may not have inherited your looks,

But your *strong will* is what I took.

Hear my Voice

January 2004

You listen to something I call "here say."
You judge others on their past and never listen to what
    they have to say.
You try to make it something that it is not,
You try to make my real friends' feelings stop.
You listen, you hear, you feel, but you don't see.
As a child, you should believe me.
I try to and I often protest,
But that just fills my heart and mind with stress.
You say that all you want me to do is confess.
I thank the Lord that I am blessed.
You say that I am making the wrong choice,
But please give me a chance and *hear my voice.*

Crying Silent Tears

February 2004

I'm crying; but no one hears, because I'm crying silent
   tears.
I'm crying; but my voice is silent,
My actions are evil and extremely violent.
I'm crying; but I have no expression,
This is the moment for my confession.
I'm crying; listen close, compassion
   and love is what I need the most.
I'm crying; but I don't know why,
I can't even look at you in the eye.
I'm crying; I feel used, I feel beaten and abused.
I'm crying; but I can't be heard, I'm in a cage trapped like
   a bird.
I'm crying long and hard;
Nothing will cheer me up not even a friendly card.
I'm crying; I feel a suffering pain,
In my heart I hope it doesn't remain.
I'm crying; but you can only see my tears, because as I said
   before
I'm *crying silent tears.*

"In God I trust; I will not be afraid. What can man do to
me?"   —Psalm 56:11

The Girl in the Mirror

March 2004

I look at this person; I see her every day.
At school at home, and when I'd go out to play.
I question this person but a response is never heard,
I try to talk to her but she doesn't say a word.
She does many things that I like to do: write poems,
Talk to friends, and she plays soccer too.
She's always there even when I don't expect her to be.
She's like the person that I dream to be.
Her grades are good and all the colleges want her.
She is what I might call a "Soccer Star".
Its like all my dreams are hers and now they seem so
    far away,
Too far to ever reach.
It's like she's taking my life and my freedom of speech.
I don't know her name or where she came from,
But I wish she would leave because she's ruining my
    life.
It's like she's trying to be me.

This person is trying to steal my identity.
How can this be? God created us to have our own
    destiny!
I can't get away from this person, it's like she's a part
    of me.
I lay down my head to fall asleep and hope that my
    dreams
Are something that I can keep.
I wake-up in the morning and there she is—

That girl in the mirror who is trying to live up to me. Then I realize that, that *girl in the mirror* is me.

"But now, this is what the Lord says—he who created you, O Jacob, he formed you, O Israel: 'Fear not, for I have redeemed you; I have summoned you by name; you are mine.'"—Isaiah 43:1

What If

March 2004

What if there was no violence in this world,
What if there were no more rapings of young innocent
   girls.
What if everybody had their own special love?
What if everyone could go to the Heavens above?
What if I asked you to marry me?
What if I was bended down on one knee?
What if to me you cheated and lied?
What if one day I just broke down and cried?
What if Courtney wasn't my name?
What if I was a star and I had money and fame?
What if I never saw you again?
What if I died, you will never know when
What if this was the last thing that I write?
What if I was like Stevie Wonder and I had no sight?
What if you told me that you were my best friend?
What if you thought of me and gave me a helping
   hand?
What if I left this world and nobody knew?
What if there was no more me or you. . .

✝

Destiny of Mine

April 2004

Every second that goes by,
Every minute of the day,
I wonder if it's my destiny to be this way.
I feel like my destiny is being chosen by another.
As I stand here today,
I'm looking like one of my brothers.

Every second that goes by,
every hour of the day,
I wonder why children say
The things that they say.
I'm feel like I'm standing in the shadow of myself,
Like I work continuously but I have no wealth.

Every second that goes by,
Every day of the week,
I wonder why dreams are dreadful
At night while I sleep.
I feel like someone doesn't want me here;
My heart beats fast as the days draw near.

Every second, every minute, all of the time,
I wonder if this is the *destiny of mine*.

"We live by faith, not by sight."
—II Corinthians 5:7

Seen by All

June 2004

Everything I do is seen by all,
When I'm in the classroom or roaming through the
    halls.
Everything I do is seen, but not really acknowledged,
I can't wait to graduate, so I can run straight off to
    college.
Everything I do is questioned with who, what, when
    and why,
Everything I do is seen in the public eye.
Every step I take is counted like I'm a criminal on the
    run,
Every move I make could be my last one.
Everything I want, somebody takes away,
Everything that's on my mind, I will strongly say.
Everything that my friends do comes back on me,
Every day when I am looked down upon, I feel like a
    slave who isn't free.
Every move I make is a struggle, despite all of my
    troubles.
I will stand tall, because everything I do is *seen by all*.

"You discern my going out and my lying down; you
are familiar with all my ways. Before a word is on my
tongue you know it completely, O Lord."

—Psalm 139: 3-4

In the Middle of it All

June 2004

I'm not really in with the "in" crowd or out with the
    "out,"
I'm not really quiet and I don't really shout.
I'm not really titled by one group at all,
That's why I consider myself *in the middle of it all.*
I know a lot about computers and how to fix things,
But I also know about life and what dedication means.
I'm not like everybody else because soccer is my game,
In this world basketball is not the only
Way you can make yourself a name.
Instead of watching the NBA I'd rather watch the MSL
If it's soccer, I'll play in the rain, sleet or hail.
I don't really want to be in a "clique"
I'd rather just be me because the "clique" won't always
Be there and life is not guaranteed.
God made an individual so I can stand on my own two
    feet,
In life there are challenges that you have to conquer
    and defeat.
I'm proud of who I am and where I've come from,
I pleased with my accomplishments
and the young woman I've become.
During my life I've been put to the rest,
My auntie took her last breath now her soul may rest.
I wouldn't have survived without my Best, Best.
To Lydia, I say "May God bless."
I feel like nothing can stop me,
Except me standing back letting my life pass by.

It's like I have a mirror and I can't even look at myself
   in the eye.
I don't really fit in with anybody, I just chill alone,
As a young child I feel like my identity is unknown.
On my own two feet I must stand tall, because as I
   said,
Before in this world I'm *in the middle of it all.*

No One Understands
June 2004

I ask you why you did it,
Why you put me in this place
Why, as a young child, all these
Problems I must face
I ask myself why and simply that
In this world I don't know where my place is at.
I ask you again and again,
Do you honestly think you're right?
If I had the chance, I would rearrange my sight,
So that I couldn't see anything
That was going on here, because
All that I see in this world,
I constantly fear.
This means nothing just
Words on a sheet.
I may write it,
But it's not always neat.
So what, I don't care and neither should you,
What I do reflects on me and not you.
I may not be famous, but I already have fans.
They may look up to me, but really,
No One Understands.

"And my God will meet all your needs according
to his glorious riches in Christ Jesus."
—Philippians 4:19

There's No Place like Hope

Dedicated to: Boys Hope Girls Hope of Detroit,
my second family
October 2004

I started on this journey to better myself in life,
But in order to do this I had to make a sacrifice.
No more cell phone or chilling with old friends,
But I'll try to make the best of this and try to fit in if I
    can.
My lifestyle has completely changed and so has my
    school,
I dress more professionally and follow different rules
I miss my friends like crazy especially Danielle,
    Alanna, Drea and Flexx,
I was forced into this world; I don't know what's going
    to happen next.
I don't fit in here at all; I wish I could leave,
Without any help from anybody in my life I'll achieve.
But I know that's not the attitude that will help me to
    get by,
At times I feel so lost all I do is sit back and cry.
This world is so dangerous it is out of control,
It's like all the haters and racist are trying to steal my
    soul.
My mom put me here because she knows I have
    potential,
But there are some things I'm ashamed of and I like to
    keep confidential.
I have a new family and many news faces.
Some of different religions and some of different races.
I love them all the same,

For the last two years of my high school life in Girls
Hope I'll remain.
I have nothing to worry about because I have a lot of
    love and support,
When I'm doing my homework or running track—my
    favorite sport.
Every single person in this program has helped me a
    lot.
So let me read off these names from the bottom to the
    top.
Andrea, Tim, and Mary, you too,
You all helped me and saw me through.
To the boys at Wildermere and my little brother,
I love the jokes you guys make from one to another.
To the house parents: Wendy, Edita and Rojgette,
I know y'all are always saying "Boys, is it your bedtime
    yet?"
To the people I live with day after day,
To each of you I have something special to say.
I'm going to start off with Akua, who gives a new word,
And all through the house "outraged" was all that was
    heard.
Next comes Sarah, who is creative as ever,
When you help me, my projects always come out
    better.
To Julie the new kid on the block,
That day you didn't get lost I was in shock
To Shanina the one who on me never gives up,
No matter what the situation you always say, "Keep
    your head up"
Now on to the girls; where should I start?
In my life I'm glad every single one of you became a

part.

Ciara, you're the youngest but you still care,

Every five minutes you change the style of your hair.

Brittany, you're silly and you always put a smile on my face.

You're a good friend, and thanks for giving me my space.

Reese you're older and you're very wise,

Even though I hid myself like I was a stranger in disguise.

To Peaches, the one who styles my hair,

You'll talk to me about anything; you don't even care.

Yeah that's right Ashley, I saved you for last,

I hope we can put our bickering in the past.

You hate on me constantly, but I don't really care,

Is it because I'm so funny or the way I where my hair?

Thanks to everybody who has influenced me,

And to everybody never who gave up on me.

I didn't think I would make it, how was I going to cope?

I'm thankful for my new family that I've found in Boys and Girls Hope.

"Family isn't about whose blood you have. It's about who you care about."

—Trey Parker & Matt Stone

The Real Me

November 2004

Nobody has seen the real me,
Because I keep it hidden deep within thee.
Nobody has seen the real me,
Because all of my true feelings I cover up and hide.
Nobody knows the real me,
Nobody takes time to see.
Nobody knows my state of confusion,
Everybody makes up this picture of me,
Which is just an illusion.
Nobody knows my dreams while I sleep,
Nobody knows the weights on my shoulders are oh so
   deep.
Nobody knows I'm a puzzle
Can you figure out the clues?
Nobody knows my information or my favorite color of
   shoes,
Nobody knows because I keep it all inside,
Hidden away from success and so much pride.
I wish that you could know me
But, I'm scared to show.
I'm to old for games open the door and come see,
My name is Courtney Elizabeth Butts and this is *the
   real me.*

A Person I Dream to Be:
Strong, Black, and Beautiful

Dedicated to Janet C. Baxter

January 2005

A person I dream to be:
Hard working, skilled and intelligent.
A person much wiser than me
A person that's been there for the last seventeen years,
A person who has stuck by my side through
My games, my projects and my tears.
Strong, black, and beautiful
Is the person I dream to be,
This person sounds unreal
Who could it be?

"What you decide on will be done,
and light will shine on your ways." —Job 22:28

Survive
January 2005

I can't spend my whole life worried about others,
I have to protect myself, but I'll still love you like a brother.
All of the stress is causing my heart pain.
These feelings inside me, I just can't explain.
I've been putting on a front, or just a little show,
But I'm getting much older, so I have to say NO!
I'm not on this earth for Rosemary or my mommy.
I'm in this world searching for myself and my true destiny.
I can give you advice, but I can't live your life,
Because I've got my own to live, filled with struggles and
    strife.
Despite all the things that have happened in the past,
I can achieve my goal first, and still be considered last.
I'm sixteen years old; I'll be seventeen in May,
I question myself daily on why I chose to be this way.
I say it's just a phase but some things you can't outgrow,
I will sit back in my thinking chair
    and wait for God to show me my true path to guide me,
I feel this is just a dream and I need to wake up and see
    reality.
For sixteen years, by God's grace, I'm still alive,
    but this is only the beginning and
Yes, I will *survive*.

"For it is God who works in you to will
and to act according to his good purpose."
                        —Philippians 2:13

Struggle to Survive

February 2005

God knew it all before I was even conceived,
He knew my complexion and the support I would need.
He threw me this world to make my mark,
I've messed up so far but my life doesn't have a restart.
I've got to keep on living because I can't give up,
Despite everything, I can't get fed up.
Sometimes I just want to break down and cry,
It's like I want to tell the truth, but out comes a lie.
So many people support me, but do often question,
Eventually it will be the moment for my confession.
God gave me my own mind and the skills to write,
And he gave me the courage to never give up the fight.
Every step that I take, the Lord already knows,
From the result of the action, it really shows.
I have so many people who come to me for advice,
But sometimes, I have to take a break and live my own life.
Sometimes when I'm hurt I question the Lord,
Is He trying to harm me like the wound from a sword?
Many people put me down as if they're better than me,
But I have my own dreams and my own destiny!
You can't hold me back because you're not stronger than
    me,
In my heart I know that "Only God Can Judge Me"
Lord, I thank you for never giving up,
My heart is full of love it just might erupt.
Nobody in my life wants to see me fail,
It's like a battle between going to Heaven or leaning
    towards Hell.

Reality

I don't need to worry about that, because God loves me,
Despite all the sins that I commit against thee.
Some people die young, and some stay alive,
But in this world, it's still a *struggle to survive.*

"If there is no struggle, there is no progress"
—Frederick Douglass

They Said I Couldn't Do It
February 2005

People told me I wasn't good enough
To even make the team,
They told me my job was to fill the water bottles
And keep the shoes clean.
But I just turned away and said to myself,
"Jesus Loves Me."
I know where I've come from, and who I plan to be.
Later on that week, I laughed at the thought...
They still said "no" after all the talent I had brought.
Despite the fight I put up,
Everybody said: "Courtney, just give up."
They told me I was a failure and that I had no luck,
But I just pray to God, because I know He loves me.
I pray that I make and give myself an identity.
The title of this poem is funny—
"They said I couldn't do it."
They say a lot,
But I know in my heart I can never be stopped!

 "The Lord is far from the wicked but he hears the
prayer of the righteous." —Proverbs 15:29

The Black Legacy

February 2005

In the 40's, 50's and 60's...hatred crossed the nation,
Blacks were beaten and killed, and there was much
　discrimination.
Just because the color of our skin, people shun away
　from us,
Look down on us, and act as if they're better than us.
I won't settle for that, because God created us all equal
　in his image.
We've overcome slavery for three hundred years,
And we're still standing tall, despite the shed of blood
　and tears.
You can beat me all you want, but you can't take away
　my pride,
Outside, you'll see a strong black woman, but I still
　have much fear inside.
All those years and all those people that didn't make it
　through,
I thank God that they did what they had to do.
No coloreds allowed; what kind of nonsense is that?
When I think of racism, all I can do is sing and clap.
Martin Luther King Jr., Rosa Parks, Malcolm X, and
　Sojourner Truth...
They led us through these tough times, not only them,
　but many others.
The white man can turn his back on me, but not on the
　African American Race,
I'm history in the making so you'd better remember
　my face.
No matter what you say to me or what you think is

right,
We will not be divided, and we'll never give up the
fight.
All we wanted were decent jobs, good pay, the right to
vote, the right to learn, respect and equality.
In the good book, it doesn't say:
"I created whites to be better than blacks,"
You can talk the talk, but not if you don't know the
facts.
We've come a long way since the days of Dr. King,
However, the fight isn't over and I say, "Let Freedom
Ring!"
We can go to school now, but we'd rather skip and
smoke weed,
And your mothers plead, trying to explain that your
ancestors fought for you.
But you treat life like it's a game or a big party
Because that's all you do,
You worry about getting laid and who out there is
better than you.
I know sometimes I do complain,
But when I die I want greatness written behind my
name.
Many county jails are full of young black brothers.
And why?
Because you beat on yo baby's mama or shot up the
store,
Smoked weed and got caught or so many things more.
And don't call yourself a leader, because you're just
following the crowd,
And look at your report card, your mother can't even
be proud.

So many opportunities are being thrown away.

Right in front of your face people are willing to pay,

Your way to college if you would just get good grades,

Throw down your guns, blunts, lighters, and blades.

Years ago, we couldn't even walk on the streets without
being questioned.

I wish that all of Africans Americans valued life the
same,

Like life is a blessing despite the suffering pain.

I value the ones, who love and protect me.

God put me here to create my own destiny,

As of 2005 this is my vision of

The Black Legacy.

"Our lives begin to end the day we become silent about
things that matter."

—Dr. Martin Luther King Jr.

Understand Me

March 2005

I'm so confused, I feel like I'm at the end of the road.
Nowhere to turn, nowhere to go.
Every time I find something good, it goes away.
Every time things are good it turns out not to go my way.
I see one person in the morning and another one at night,
When I look in the mirror, I can't decide which one is right.
God help me to find myself and the purpose for my life,
I will always worship You for making a sacrifice.
I feel like I'm at the crossroads with so many options,
So many choices, so many destinies
Nobody really knows, but they think they do.
They think they know me but they don't have a clue
    what is going on "Inside My Head"
What burdens lie in my heart while I'm sitting in my bed.
I go on and on and write poems day after day.
But this is my only way to express myself in my own special
    way.
I feel like my voice is quiet because nobody really hears
    me.
Lord, you see me struggling so please help me.
In 2005 I'm still struggling to see,
Why nobody in this world understands me.

"I am not ashamed of the gospel, because it is the power of
God for the salvation of everyone who believes." —Romans
1:16a

✝

Just Sit and Listen

Inspired by: Marian High School students
May 2005

I was sitting there as you talked about me.
Although, you didn't notice me.
The smile on my face disappeared,
Replaced with a tear
From the pain that you caused,
But, to you, I applaud.
You said your true feelings.
They put a wound in my heart,
Yet I'm still blessed that, in my life, you became a part.
Instead of hating you for the words that you said,
I will bend down on my knees and bow my head.
Dear God,
    Help me and the ones that surround,
    To understand that you're still around.
    Words do hurt any way they are used.
    It could be from talk of sex or a child that was
      abused.
    Although you hurt me, you're still my friend
    In Jesus' name I pray,
    Amen.
Now if I was a hateful person and I held a grudge,
And I am sitting here thinking that, by you, I could be
    judged.
But that's not me I have no reason to hate on you,
Or your opinion, or the assumptions you make.
I let your words get to me when I should have brushed
    them off,
Don't take me lightly because this kid isn't soft.

I look back at yesterday, now that it is all over,
And I still feel pain, but it's not all the same.
I can't look at you like I did before,
I look at you like a child, judging me for what I wore
To the party last week,
Or like a friend who questions the way that I speak.
It's funny how my joy can quickly turn bad,
What kind of friend would make me so mad?
I have one final question, which one of us is wrong?
I will *just sit and listen*, left all alone.

"Do not judge, or you too will be judged. For in the
same way you judge others, you will be judged, and
with the measure you use, it will be measures to you."
—Matthew 7: 1-2

Diploma in My Hand

Dedicated to: Marian High School
Boys Hope Girls Hope of Detroit
July 2006

I stood there in my white robe, diploma in my hand.

Trying to figure out if this night had really began.

Pictures flashing, tears flowing as everyone enjoyed this
    night.

I kept thinking to myself, "This can't be right."

I'm trying to rewind my mind back to the days that I
    remember

To our flag football game in late September.

Or maybe farther back than that—back to my first field day,

I had do clue; all we had to do was play.

I remember my first mass and listening to the priest,

He spoke about new beginnings and the Thanksgiving
    feast.

In the beginning of the year, I was so confused.

I remember A & B lunches;

during free hour which one would I choose?

I remember my first detention for standing up for what I
    believe,

And I remember watching the clock waiting for the time to
    leave.

Now the time has come when we will not return,

We've proudly expressed all of our fears and all of our
    concerns.

We've had all the tests and completed all the tasks,

Now we're leaving behind a great legacy and past.

As I walked across the stage, with my diploma in my hand,

I remembered my mother's words: "Courtney, I know you
  can."
Four years of my life is now behind me,
And I'm striving to be the best in what lies before me.
I stood there in my white robe, *diploma in my hand,*
Thanking God for creating me as a part of His plan.

At Age Fourteen
March 2003

Fourteen years old and my auntie just died,
I felt like forever I could have cried.

Grades started to drop lower than B's
And my friends help me re-create my identity.

Sundays at church were no joy for me,
Because I felt like I had no reason to breathe.

I didn't read scripture or listen to the Word,
The most important thing to me was the next
   Rap song to be heard.

I'd rather walk the halls than get an education,
Who ever thought I would major in religion and
   communications?

Hanging in the streets was the life I sought,
Air Force 1's ® and headbands was all I bought.

Nobody in this world was good enough for me,
I found myself upset by the way others looked at me.

So many secrets and so many lies,
So many things I had not realized.

Fourteen years, trying to find myself,
I felt like to be important I needed popularity and
   wealth.

All the things that I used to wish for and used to
    believe,
Are now just thoughts and childish dreams.

Ending this year in denial and with regrets,
Whose fault is it that I'm so upset?

At fourteen years old I never thought I'd make it to
    college,
Or think the Bible could give me so much guidance and
    knowledge.

Fourteen years old and my auntie just died,
I lost my determination and all of my pride.

"Let another praise you, and not your own mouth;
someone else, and not your own lips." —Proverbs 27:2

My Legacy

Dedicated to Boys Hope Girls Hope of Detroit
August 2006

I came into this program at age sixteen,
I was shy, quiet and some would say mean.
I struggled in high school and I felt all alone,
But in Girls Hope I found myself a new home.
22 months of my life was spent here,
To excel in school and conquer my fears.
As I move away from this place and travel off to
     college,
I've been nurtured with much wisdom and knowledge.
I'm thankful for this program and I'm thankful for this
     chance,
As a freshman in college I take a second glance
At what I leave behind and what lies before me,
I leave behind friends, family and what Girls Hope has
     been to me.
In school I leave behind old friends that looked up to
     me,
Teammates and classmates that always encouraged
     me.
In the hallways I'm leaving my memory,
I made it through despite those who tried to break my
     dignity.
In the community I'm leaving my dedication,
Hoping that others will follow in my attempts of
     participation.
I try to give back like others have done for me,
My work in this world is what is expected of me.
My family is my mom she's the one that completes me,

I leave behind much love for her and much generosity.
I leave behind a promise that I will make it in this
world,
I'm determined to make her proud because I'm her
little girl.
To my second family that has molded me into who I
am,
I leave behind my legacy as well as a diploma in my
hand.
I'm leaving behind the person that I have grown to be,
Hoping that others will be as dedicated as me.
As you remember how I have grown, remember how I
used to be,
Thank you for the self-confidence that you have
endured in me.
I leave behind a child, who was never supposed to
make it,
A child, who didn't know herself so she was just trying
to fake it.
A child, who was never supposed to have,
What I have or seen what I've seen.
This world was trying to corrupt my mind
And make my thoughts unclean.
It's like I was desiring to do nothing more than this
with my life,
But I thank God I was given a second chance at life.
A life of hope and a life of success.
I know that in my life I have truly been blessed.
When thinking about this program it wasn't always
good,
But I know that keeping a peaceful mind is something
I should

Do to make it better when things don't seem right,
Us girls do sometimes argue but for one another we
will always fight.
I used to think there was no place like home
But now I know "there's no place like hope,"
Where there's always someone willing to help you
cope.
I'm not going to end this with a quote or a little cliché,
I will end this by simply saying, this is my legacy and
remember me this way.

College Success, 2006

Who I Am

2006

I know what you're thinking... At first, she didn't know,
    and now she does?
I can change my mind and I feel this way because I know
    who I am: Courtney Elizabeth Butts.
As an ordinary person, you would think, "So what?
In just a couple of years what could really change?"
My mind, my actions and even the way I complain.
In my mind, I've been transformed regarding the way I
    think,
And I'm more careful with thinking before I speak.
Who am I?
I'm a shining star; in what I used to believe,
    my knowledge has come so far.
I'm a child who is searching for her purpose in life,
    determined to serve others
And always willing to make a sacrifice for the ones that I
    live for.
I love my friends a lot, but my mom even more.
Who am I?
A child who's blessed, and was ready at the moment
I had to confess all of my sins unto the Lord.
Now I worship proudly with my church in one accord.
I have a great idea of the person I want to be,
    and as I continue to live, I'll grow into what I see.
This is a decision I have to make all by myself.
A couple of years ago I didn't know what, with my life,
    I wanted to do.
I was living my life like a child without a clue.

Reality

You'll probably question me as you read this,
    but I just have one question for you.
I know who I am, but who are you?

Closing Prayer

Dear Heavenly Father,

I come to You with all my sins, my burdens and addictions. Wash me in the precious blood that Jesus shed for me when He died on the cross. Break the chains of sin and of satan in my life and family. I surrender to You and I want to be Yours—spirit, soul and body, for time and eternity. I put my faith in You alone, Lord Jesus Christ. You are the only begotten Son of the Living God. I believe with my heart what I now confess with my mouth: You are my Savior, Lord and God. My sins are now forgiven and I have been "born-again!" Old things have passed away and I am a new creation in Christ Jesus. I am a child of God. I believe it and I receive it in the mighty name of Jesus Christ of Nazareth.

AMEN.[2]

[2](Bible.com 1994-2005 ©)

About the Author

C OURTNEY BUTTS' interest in writing began in 6th grade at Detroit Open School. At age fourteen Courtney performed, "I Want to Be Just Like You" and dedicated that performance to her mother at her 8th grade graduation. In 2003 Courtney's writing was enhanced through the Inside Out Poetry club at Mumford High School. There she began to develop a collection of poetry as she journeyed through her adolescent years. Courtney has been featured in many poetry night events across the Metro Detroit area. She enjoys writing, photography, playing sports, spending time with family and has a great sense of humor. She is currently a sophomore at Indiana Wesleyan University, majoring in Social Work. Courtney is Christ centered and is motivated to serve others. Courtney believes she is being lead by God to "stand out" as it says in His word: "I knew you before I formed you in your mother's womb. Before you were born I set you apart and appointed you as my prophet to the nations." (NLT)

To order additional copies of *Inside My Head*, or to find out about other books by Courtney E. Butts or Zoë Life Publishing, please visit our website www.zoelifepub.com.

A bulk discount is available when 12 or more books are purchased at one time.

Contact Outreach at Zoë Life Publishing:

Zoë Life Publishing
P.O. Box 871066
Canton, MI 48187
(877) 841-3400
outreach@zoelifepub.com